"Andi Penner's poetry is a cause for celebration. Her real genius lies in capturing the small, often unnoticed and imperfect life events and describing them perfectly. Whether it's a phone call with a friend, a trip to a bakery or the raw emotion felt after listening to an NPR interview, Penner is wise, poignant and funny. This book is a must-read for anyone who wants to be reminded of what's important in life."

Eddi Porter, Learning & Development Team Leader,
BP America/North America Gas

"Reading these poems today was like a pause to refresh myself in something deep and still. I felt I was a voyeur of a very observant mind, listening to it process the experiences of real life, watching it contemplate a simple view and allowing me to touch it with my fingertips, so earthy in the most sensuous way. The poet's thoughts and observances reflect beautifully a deep, enlivened stillness. Childhood, mothers, home...the vagaries of the divorce conundrums... and her 'noticings' of bits of life. They all touched me."

Nancy Washburn, Professor of Child and Family Studies,
Los Angeles City College

Nov. 2013
Albuq.

When East Was North

for Juanita ~
a fellow poet &
fellow Sandian ☺

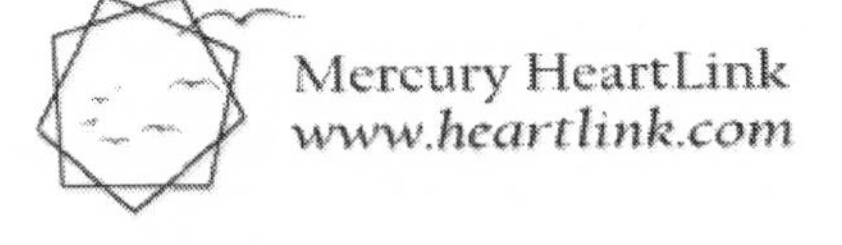

♡ Andi

When East Was North

Andrea Millenson Penner

When East Was North

ISBN: 978-0-9882279-6-5
Publisher: Mercury HeartLink
Albuquerque, New Mexico
Printed in the United States of America

Photographs of the author taken by
Madison Burr Photography, Albuquerque, New Mexico.

Contact: *pennerink@gmail.com*

Acknowledgments

Several poems in this collection have appeared previously, some in slightly different form, in the following publications: "Coming Across" and "February Snow," *Epiphany*; "I-40 Construction Zone," *Conceptions Southwest*; "Forbidden Fruit Jam," "New Mexico Directions," "Peace Talks," "Recipe," and "Vera in Two Snapshots," *Illumina*.

The cover artwork, "Shower of Stars on the Rio Grande," was generously provided by Meg Leonard, Placitas, New Mexico. Please visit: *www.megleonard.com*.

Thank you, Stewart, for your publishing midwifery. Many thanks to Andrea Kristina's Bookstore & Kafé in Farmington, New Mexico, a wonderful venue for writing, discussing, and reading poetry. I am also grateful to the audiences who listened to many of my works-in-progress.

POEMS

I. IN MY OWN INK

II. THE WRITER'S ASANA

III. NIGHT SPACES

IV. BUT NOT TODAY

V. FORBIDDEN FRUIT JAM

For Dad, Laura, and Jeff, there from the beginning.
For Erin and Avram, mapping their own directions.
And for Keith, my East, South, West, and North.

I.

Once at a Basque beach café in northern Spain, I ordered Chipirones en su Tinta: *Squid in its own Ink.*

We, too, are prepared and served in our own ink – clouded by memory, inscribed by the past.

IN MY OWN INK

California: Two Haiku

Eucalyptus leaves
fall
        silently....
                                        Spiral spears
through coastal fog.

Coastal fog enshrouds
draping fennel, pampas, gum
salty silence falls.

From Point Conception to the Mexican Border

As we sped southward
toward San Diego
on a Saturday morning,
we heard the familiar Southland weather forecast in male
monotone: "night and early morning low clouds
and fog along the coast, from Point Conception
to the Mexican border, today and tomorrow."

We paid little attention to the music, and
even less to the newscast
absorbed in our favorite car games:
Alphabet, Jotto, Geography.

Suddenly, my ears smiled:
"Equis, E, Ere, A
Tijuana, Mexico!"
The station identification X-E-R-A
rolled onto the airwaves
in a woman's sexy Spanish.

Her lilting rhythm
awoke my childhood imagination
to the world beyond the border.
I had heard her voice many times
on border blaster radio, but that day,
as we crossed the bridge into Baja
I half-expected to see her—
brown shoulders, red lips
large hoop earrings
flashing through dark hair
singing the call letters

"Equis, E, Ere, A
Tijuana, Mexico!"

We entered a
crowd of bustling tourists
and hustling locals
who swept us down the street
into a colorful sea of crepe paper poppies
embroidered blouses, and tooled leather purses.
I held my father's hand, remotely aware of his presence,
transfixed by large brown eyes meeting my own—
not those of the mysterious radio woman
but of children singing "*Chicle, chicle*" shaking boxes
of tiny confetti-colored chewing gum like maracas.

A Cold War Childhood

Garden Drive, the cul-de-sac
    center of my world,
    where east was north in my mind map.
    Safely surrounded by orange groves and strawberry fields
    city parks and libraries
    second-hand stores on Main Street.

Our house, remodeled
    with French doors and bay windows
    and a doggy door, just my size
    places to play troll dolls
    and whisper secrets.

The yard, tended by Mr. Shishedo,
    whom I followed around and called "Mr. Muh-sheedo,"
    where roses, azaleas, gardenias, camellias,
    and miniature citrus trees
    competed with the double-trunked wonder that bore
both plums and apricots.

School, on yellow busses
    Talented and gifted,
    we learned our lessons
    despite red threats, smog alerts, and
    duck-and-cover drills—
    learned, that even here, leaders are assassinated.

Weekends free, on stingray bikes
we pedaled to the miniature golf course
or snuck out the back of the bowling alley
    and into Disneyland, our surreal playground
    where we begged E-tickets from unsuspecting tourists

and argued about the revolving Carousel of Progress—
    was it the stage or the audience?

The garage, where Dad spent repeated rounds
of Aerospace layoffs
and haunted his shop
organizing tools on white pegboard painted
with red outlines of hammers and saws
beneath slogans like
"Wear Goggles: The Eyes You Save May Be Your Own."

Inside, Mom kept the peace
    with tollhouse cookies and a clean kitchen.
    She prepared chicken soup with matzo balls
    while humming arias and daydreaming.
During dinner,
    Walter Cronkite's steady voice
    reassured us all.

Feeling Lucky

Between songs, the KEZY d.j., Mr. Wonderful,
announced that he was broadcasting live
from a Suzuki dealership.

Mr. Wonderful was our friend Jerry
whom mom had met
in a night class.
He and my sister did community theater together,
so we all felt like celebrities, knowing the man behind the voice.

When Jerry said
they would be giving away a motorcycle,
Mom announced: "I feel lucky tonight."

We followed her into the bedroom,
plopped on her bed, and watched her get ready.

She selected a lime green and white ensemble
with matching pumps and dangly white hoops.
She applied fresh black eyeliner and
bright orangey-pink lipstick, making faces at herself
in the mirror as she opened, puckered, and blotted.
Finally, she spritzed herself
with Estee Lauder "Beautiful,"
kissed us each carefully on the cheek,
and wafted into the evening
calling out, "Be good."

The three of us separated into our own summer worlds—
Laura talked on the phone, Jeff disappeared into a book, and I
played solitaire.

At 8:00 o'clock we shushed each other and held our breaths as
Mr. Wonderful announced the winner... FRED HOBBS

We couldn't believe it. There must be some mistake.

When Fred didn't appear, Jerry drew again:
MARLENE MILLENSON
Mom won!

I wanted her to roar up on a big black chopper,
but only a little beige motorbike was delivered sometime later
and quickly sold.

1968

After school
after homework
Jeff and I would set the table
before Laura came home from cheerleading practice
    or school play rehearsal.

We collected the everyday china plates,
salad bowls, silverware, and glassware—
    five of each
and placed them just so
in front of each maple chair.
(Dad's was the Captain's chair, with arms.)

Jeff taught me to fold the napkins into fans.
    (He had read a book about how to do this.)

Mom's veal parmesan or beef burgundy already
bubbled in the oven
    filling the kitchen with spicy warmth
    while she cut fresh green beans to place in the steamer
    and mixed melted butter, crushed garlic for the bread.
Jeff carried the scissors outside.
    I followed him to the back yard
    or the front patio
    with a basket
    to catch the flowers.

Inside, we created the centerpiece
    gardenias and camellias floating in a crystal bowl
    roses arranged in a white milk glass vase.

Then we made the salad, raiding the refrigerator
for all the ingredients from the local produce stand:
romaine, avocadoes, tomatoes, cucumbers,
mushrooms, celery—
carefully washing the vegetables
and cutting off the ends
as we were told.
For the finishing touch, we added black olives
and sprinkled the top with bacon bits or croutons
before placing the wooden salad fork and spoon
on either side.

So much preparation
as though the food was
an offering
set carefully
upon the dining room altar.

Our silent, desperate prayer.

New Mexico Directions

Take 40 west to 131,
Cañoncito exit
to stop sign.
Make a right.
Past the store, trading post, post office.
Cross the bridge,
next turn off,
after cattle guard,
make a right onto dirt road.
You'll see the church.
Then a quick left up the hill.
Stay to the left at the fork
or you'll end up in the arroyo.
Down the hill, make a right at the post
with house numbers on it.
Stay on the middle road, the one between
the hogan and the house,
until you get to the last house where the road ends.
Oh yeah—go past the corral.
You'll see the house number—39.
See you sometime.

D.J.

He was one of only three or four black kids at my high school,
and three grades behind me.
Unlikely friends, all we had in common was football.
D.J. liked the game;
I liked watching the boys who played it.
That was the year the Argonauts played for Jesus.
The God squad didn't lose games
and the cheerleaders didn't lose anything, either.

After school
in late fall
D.J. and I boarded a booster bus
and traveled from suburb to city
for a district playoff game,
bouncing on hard green seats
and shouting school slogans.
Somehow united in Argo pride,
we all yelled cheers like
    Jack their heads, Big Red,
    Jack their heads!

We disembarked,
crossing a crowded parking lot teeming with high school kids—
blacks and whites, Asians and Chicanos.
Girl cliques paraded in crop tops and hip huggers
followed by boys in bell bottoms and puka shells.
Long hairs disappeared under the bleachers
to get high or get laid.
Groups of rival fans in varsity jackets
cracked jokes and laughed obnoxiously,
arms slung over shoulders.

D.J. swayed through the swirl
of talk, nods, and gestures,
his sly smile reserved only for the coolest.
I held his hand.

"Hey, buy me a program," he ordered
as we approached the stands.
"I don't have any more money, D.J."
"Okay, then," he said. "Be a Jew."

I dropped his hand,
grabbed his shoulder,
and said, "I am."

"Oh," he whispered.

Returning to the high school, the bus vibrated
with another victory,
but D.J. and I were quiet.
"I'm sorry," he said as we stepped off the bus.
"It's okay. Want a ride home? My Mom can drive you."
"No thanks. I'll walk."

My mother wondered at his reluctance to ride with us.
I couldn't explain.

Casita Amarilla

After buying my house
in Farmington
I wrote to a friend in North Carolina
to share the news.

I could picture him and his family
in their two-story white forever home
reading the mail delivered by a postal carrier
who had crossed emerald green lawns
and stepped carefully along lily-lined walkways
who smiled to toddlers on tricycles
and barking Labradors on leashes.

My little yellow house,
I began,
sits at the southern edge of town on a flat expanse
terraced above the river valley.

From beneath the apricot tree
in my overgrown backyard,
I look across alfalfa fields, below,
and past the distant cottonwood trees
gracing the banks of the San Juan
to the bluffs—
a series of sandstone mesas
concealing canyons of rock art, fossil remains,
the ruins of ancient stone and adobe dwellings,
and crumbling hogans.
One rock spire appears
in the late afternoons
as the sun transverses
between spring and autumn equinoxes.

Its phallic shadow grows tall against the massive layers.
On the far horizon,
the silhouette
of a crenelated mesa
serrates the expansive sky.

Geese invade the valley in loud Vs
frightening the wild turkeys
into a frenzy of gobbles.
A lone red tail hawk lives nearby. Occasionally
she bursts forth from atop the closest cottonwood
screaming after her prey.
More often she soars silently
riding a thermal.

At night,
I sit in the dark—
coyotes sing
to the waning moon
while I squint at the Pleiades
and inhale the dry stillness.
This is my house, my life.
With love.

One day, the reply arrives.
I envy how you describe your house,
he says.
Here, people brag about
yards and pools
and public schools.
They compare square footage
and stainless steel appliances.

But in the west,
the landscape is your home—
the house
          simply an excuse.

Vera, in Two Snapshots

I.
My mother's elegant, fountain-pen script glides across
the back of the small, square snapshot
"Swopes and Millensons / Simsbury, Conn. 1961"
Early spring in black and white—
young mothers and their children
posing in the grassy space between two houses
amid scattered blankets and playthings—
a small, twiggy tree in the background.

Surrounded by the brood, you smile slightly, Vera,
daughters in your arms, the younger, rubbing her eye—
the other leaning into you, with one hand on her doll.
Behind you, my brother and sister smile, gap-toothed
faces poking from around your shoulders.

Your friend and next-door neighbor, my mother, sits to
your left
with me melting into her lap.
I am the youngest, shy and ever serious.
My mother's smile flirts with the camera—
Her head, tilted slightly.
Her hand in mid-air has just touched
her hair.

The image cannot tell me who was behind the camera
nor whether the little valise on the lawn was the one I packed
when we moved far away to California
that summer.

II.
Autumn reunion—1979.
My mother wrote of my visiting a friend who went to Vassar.
You invited us for dinner at 6:00 p.m.
A stranger, I stroll up the driveway of 24 Wescott Road,
distracted by vivid colors of a Connecticut fall, until I see you, Vera,
framed by the woods down the street.

Your right hand waves a friendly hello
Your left arm bears grasses and flowers—

a burning image of
browns, rusts, and yellows
draped across your olive-green knit sweater.

Your cheeks, lips, and hair glow
in lingering autumn light.

III.
Now, years later in a new century, I find the old photograph and wonder.
Had we stayed,
would I have gotten to know you, sat on your lap, trusted you with family secrets?
Had we stayed,
would I know the names of the grasses you carried, and know how to weave them into table wreaths?
Had we stayed,
would my mother radiate health and vigor
instead of being trapped in diseased, rigid silence
unable to lift a pen or brush
her cropped, gray hair?
I think of you, Vera.
And I wonder.

Assisted Living

First, I gave the yogurt maker
and the air-popped popcorn popper
to a friend.

Then at the garage sale
I sold the Japanese sesame seed grinder,
the Kitchen Aid Mixmaster,
and the simple stitch Singer sewing machine (despite protests
from my daughter
who had never before shown an interest in sewing).
Quick to disappear from the sale table were the
small round GE waffle iron, the Corning Ware electric skillet
and the egg nog set she redeemed with S & H green stamps
at an Albuquerque gas station in the fifties.

A neighbor wanted the heavy old steam iron
for her children's craft projects,
so I threw in the green plastic lettuce spinner
and a pair of old walking shoes.

The hair dryer and its companion, the seldom-used curling iron,
remained hidden under the bathroom sink
behind the cool-mist humidifier until the move,
at which point they all landed in the

Please Take box
on her front porch.

Also in that box were the 12-cup
Norelco coffee maker (minus carafe),
the Water Pic oral hygiene device,
a cassette player without its cord,

and the white bagel-sized toaster
with red and green plastic-bag ink
melted to its side.

We moved her with only a few china cups and saucers
from her collection,
her bottle of "Beautiful,"
her lilac hand lotion and favorite lipstick,
the framed photographs of her grandchildren,
and the lacquered lingerie dresser
        full of cotton nightgowns and socks.

All the essentials
of assisted living.

Living Will

There you lie, Mom,
stretched out and rigid in your adjustable bed
at home
breathing, staring
occasionally blinking
morphine pump sending pain
relief through your bloodstream to your brain
awake   sometimes   asleep
neck twisted and bent
                    at an unnatural angle
        your head falls sideways and down.

After your last emergency room visit
you were brought home with oxygen
circulating through a clear plastic artery.

Now that they've inserted a feeding tube,
your caring angel, Azucena, no longer worries
that you will choke
on your liquid diet.

Instead, she bathes you with loving attention
chattering to you softly
while her telenovella keeps her company.
When I call, she quickly activates the speakerphone
so you can hear my voice
while you lie there, mom,
somehow willing yourself present,
your heart beating to a rhythm no one else can sense.

A Visit with the Dying

Just this,
nothing more.
No gift
but this simple visit.
We bring only ourselves.

You will hear our familiar voices
and try to recall our names.

As you labor to inhale,
some barely perceptible scent
will trigger your memory of us as children
and you will leave us
            temporarily
for that other time and place
closing your eyes
against the disease,
against pain.

When you open them again
focused only on our faces
you will not see the bounty of bouquets
or the "H-A-P-P-Y-B-I-R-T-H-D-A-Y" chain of letters
strung like sparkly paper dolls above the fireplace
or the cake frosted white with pink roses.

Nor will you understand
why you are still among the living.

We have come, Mom.
Now it is time
to go.

February Snow

All day
the noisy rain has been rattling the roof
dripping down the rusty drains
sploshing into muddy puddles.

Tuned to the constant hum of our old refrigerator,
the downpour beats a background rhythm
for domesticity.

Later,
after the children
have brushed their teeth
and asked for one last drink of water
after the wood stove's roar
has settled to a glowing purr
after the dishes have been washed
and sit dripping in the drain,

I hear the silence
the stillness
of white.

Monday's List

Dishes to wash
Bread to bake
Dinner to fix
Bed to make

Fruit to buy
Rent to pay
Laundry to wash

All today?

II.

Writing for me is like childbirth—
there's something deep inside me
that must be born into the world.

- Jennifer Pierce Eyen

The Writer's Asana

English 139

Lecture lost on college freshman
    vacant eyes
no exit

Take notes
            pretend
            while the rain
            drips from eucalyptus
            leaves
            outside the open window
            tapping a rhythm
            for one foot
            then the other
            then the pencil
against the desk

Body shifts
            chair squeaks
            drone continues

Hand moves toward face
            rests on cheek
            supports the head
            the weight

of empty words.

I Write

I write
short
          loose lines

because my hand goes numb
if I grip
          too tightly
or type for too long.

I write in snapshots
because my mind
photographs
its memories
for Anne Lamott's
one-inch picture
frame that holds only
so much color, line
and shadow.

I write myself
into a corner
with nowhere
else to go but
there
where
I must stay
until I write
myself out
again

again because
out of things to say
or else to go nowhere
but there
here.

I write beneath the flannel night
and into the denim pocket of the afternoon.

I write
sideways in my journal with an unquiet mind in child pose

the writer's asana.

A Teacher's Lessons

An unexpected snowstorm supplies a good excuse
for students
and teachers
          to procrastinate.

Responding to essays always takes longer than you think,
but it's never as painful as you've anticipated.

A misplaced glass of merlot leaves an indelible mark
on a student's draft.

"Five hundred words" to a teacher
means a draft of one thousand, craftily edited.
"Five hundred words" to a student
means two-hundred-and-fifty fluffed, puffed, and stuffed
with unnecessary verbiage.

When students are easily discouraged, they disappear.

What's on their minds as they walk into the classroom
differs vastly from what's on mine.

He falls asleep in class, not because he's lazy, but because
he works the graveyard shift so he can go to school full time
while still providing for his family.

She's ever late, but only because she trades babysitting with another
young mother-student. They meet in the parking lot
          between classes
to transfer kids, car seats, and diaper bags.

MLA format intimidates them as much as the gym's weight-training machines intimidate me.

Applied mathematics:
1/3 of the students suffering the death of a loved one
before 1/2 of the semester is over
equals 1 class on a downward slope toward zero.

Some mornings, coffee is not enough.

Note from a Friend

I read your poems last night,
then I went to a class.

Life Skills.

The letter S never
seemed to be more important.

Dark Flowers

Nov. 12, 2005

Spun in a tornado's wake
          a young mother of three waits in line—
an infant mouthing her shoulder,
a toddler balanced on her hip, crying,
a little boy hugging her knees.

A world away
French youths torch cars,
electrocuted into action,
jackets pulled tight against
driving rain and poverty.

Jordanian protestors raise voices and fists
against suicide bombers,
their Muslim sister and brothers.

Homeless Pakistanis huddle in frozen fear, starving
numb with loss and disbelief
at earth's violent trembling.

Angry Liberians dispute election results
as the first African woman head of state
proclaims her victory.

Afghani man has murdered his young wife,
the poet Nadia Anjuman.
Today, in the streets, her book
Dark Flower, sells volumes.

I turn off the morning news and stumble outside.
In my back yard

a single sunflower blooms
called forth by warmth
on this cloudless late autumn day,
she crowns a tall leafy stalk studded with a dozen buds poised
to join her
in one glorious yellow burst.

While the universe expands
          creating space
for our infinite sorrows
poets live, and die, to fling words like stars
and embrace hope.

Recipe

Go ahead—
use this facial masque
and you will not be tempted
    to answer the door,
    pick up the phone,
    or go outside.

Measure ½ c. oats.
Combine with ½ c. hot water.
Set aside.
Separate an egg
contemplate   what to do with the yolk
    while you
drop
    the white
        into a blender
        or a bowl.

Add 2 T. plain yogurt—any fat content.

Blend softened oats, egg white, and yogurt.
Stir in a spoonful of honey.

Glance at your journal.

Carry the potion to the bathroom
and carefully spread it on your
forehead and nose, cheeks and chin
in slow circles.

Wash your hands.
Refrigerate the surplus.

Set the kitchen timer for 15 minutes,
or 20, if you're brave.

Now, sit and write.

Record the details of this day—
the birdsong that returns
after the trash trucks and lawnmowers
have ravaged the neighborhood's quiet

the slow summer heat that slides through window screens.

Or list your writing projects—
the poem honoring your lover
or remembering your mother;

the short story about that Southern California September
when the Santa Anas blew so hot that you wore
your white cotton slip as a dress to elementary school
and you felt secretly, deliciously naked;

the letter to your father—the one you'll never send
because

....
the timer rings,
interrupting your first writing moment in weeks.

The egg has drawn tight,
the yogurt has dried,
and oat flecks
fall to the table as your fingers find your forehead.

Wash your face.
Pat it dry
        savoring its sweet softness.

Tomorrow
beat
the yolk.

Do Their Diaries Read Like Mine?

Surely I am the only one who pens
"We have been fighting for weeks
it seems, amid life's stresses"
    and on another page confesses
"We continue to struggle
in our marriage—(will we ever not?!)—
about issues both big and small
from sex and money
to clutter and making beds."

Is every married woman
    relieved when her husband
    is away
    all Saturday
    so she can write
"Today I had a feeling of lightness.
He was gone
and I didn't have to wonder what
time he'd be home for lunch
or what kind of mood he'd be in"?

Do other wives
    steal time alone
    by journaling in the bathroom
    door locked
    so they can bleed on paper
    these words:
"Yesterday, after our conversation,
I went into the laundry room and cried so hard
that twice I almost vomited"?

And does any other mother
    ache for her
    three-year-old daughter
    who overhears the fighting?
Of that day, my journal tells me
"She witnessed the whole thing—
he was very angry with me,
yelled at me, and of course I cried.
I overheard her in the kitchen: 'Don't yell at mommy.
She's a nice lady and she has a baby in her tummy.'"

Cottonwoods for Cornelia

Yesterday, Raven circled high above Paraje
a dark wheeling and dipping form
skimming low, his black eye unblinking
focused on the winged dancers
   Bluebird and Macaw
   with two Corn Maidens
Wind from the East carried sand and dust
   and the sounds of rattle, chant, and drum.

Turquoise, White Shell, and
Corn Pollen
for sale.

Today, your text message:
   Driving home now. He's passed.

Rabbits dart ahead of me
on the foothills path
Chamisa, Chocolate Flower
Rice Grass

Prickly Pear
Snakeweed
Juniper
Quail call to one another

Winterfat
Navajo Tea
Scrub Oak
Snake sunning on the climbing trail

Pinon
Soft gray feathers, scattered
Sandy wash
Two bright yellow Cottonwoods

Granite boulders – prayer places in the Sun
Tears and
Quiet sadness
Under Sky's blue canopy.

Sparrows

I find their strong basket-home
under the juniper tree,
broken shell
clinging to its nursery.

Cradling the nest
I see
    not God
but Sparrows
count the hairs
from my head—
    stray brown and gray curls
woven with twigs and colored thread
into a fragile avian bed.

Punctuation, Period.

It's a dot,
The size of a period.
In a gland the size of a tennis ball.
(Roundness.)
The world in a microspot.
Is that 10-point or 12-point font?
Bold or regular?
How big IS a speck of cancer?

I saw its shadow one night.
As we soaked in the hot tub.
The dimmed lights cast a shadow on your lungs—
Your own chin's shadow, spread darkly over your chest—
And I knew, something.

Everything and nothing changed today.
Now we know.
That's all.
We know everything and nothing.
All we can know is tied up in a little
Black knot:
As small as a Helvetica (period)
As insignificant as one speck of black
Pepper on your scrambled eggs.

My students used to ask,
"What difference does punctuation make?"

III.

...and doubtless it is true that to live a thing and
simultaneously understand it
is impossible...

- Cynthia Herrmann

Night Spaces

Ten Percent Chance

The small cold nodule on my thyroid gland
could be cancer. I'll find out today's biopsy results
on Thursday or Friday or Monday

or whenever my doctor returns to her office
and phones. Meanwhile, I rest on the couch
savoring the bittersweet chocolate

and dried Montmorency cherries Kimberly brought
me. Tomorrow I'll shower away the blue
dye, go to work, and live ninety-

percent certain that I am not the one in ten.

One Undergraduate's Angst

Santa Barbara, 1976

I.

churning chaotically, my mind works itself
into a state of confusion.

coherent thoughts struggle to surface
momentarily
out of the bubbling mire
only to be absorbed by clouds of doubt
which nearly stifle every rumination.

all is a blur—
nothing concrete on which to grasp
unable to concentrate and think clearly,
I abandon the whole process.

II.

all night I waited
        for a poem
  waited
        for a creative moment
  waited
        for my head and hands
        to pen the words
        my heart ached to make known
  waited
        and cried
        collapsing over my notebook

III.
the remaining stars flicker
while mist rises from the field of fennel
quiet light casts its spell

greeting the dawn are the crickets, birds, and I.
          they are cheerful,
but I am numb
          from the cold
          and lack
          of sleep.

Dreaming Home

I.
Exhausted
I took a nap
and dreamed about driving on the rez;
but I wasn't driving—Luci was.

From the back seat
I tried to tell her which roads to take to get me home
but the words refused to speak direction.
I couldn't even really remember where I lived.

Then her windshield was completely covered with snow or ash.
She strained through the swath cut by the lone wiper blade;
we were surrounded by gray.
I woke up in a panic.
I couldn't get home.

II.
Last night
or this morning, early
I dreamed that I was wrapped in wool
outside
alone.
I was not exactly walking, nor standing still.
Somehow, I was moving through dark cold space
my feet just inches above the sidewalk.
Someone approached me and spoke.
When I didn't respond, he commented to another Someone
that I must be one of the Homeless Ones.

I tried to say
I wasn't; I was merely out for a walk.
But then I looked down at myself,
suspended, and wondered.

I woke up, shivering,
pulled the blanket closer
trying not to panic.
Where will I go
tomorrow?

I-40 Construction Zone

In the night spaces

I hear their distant rumbling
...da-ta-ta-ta – da-ta-ta-ta...

Yellow machines
claw concrete   drive dirt
mold mountains of resurrected road
the last reverberating syllable of movement
a faint whisper of change.

Waiting, breathing
I gather strength
while dogs gnaw old bones
and jets eat the sky,
stealing the steady slow sounds of highway progress
until   again
...da-ta-ta-ta – da-ta-ta...
da-ta-ta-ta – da-ta-ta...

Blood pulsing with envy,
I am alive with tense desire
tearing tangled trees from their roots—
Make room   make room
I am   coming   climbing
carving my design   into the already scarred desert
Da-Ta-Ta – Da-Ta-Ta-Ta-Ta-Ta

THREADBARE

My ancient chenille robe
with its torn threads,
frayed
edges,
and inter-
           rupted seams

cannot protect
against elemental
anger
fear
passion

Chilled
tired

clinging
to threadbare
dis-
           repair,

I am worn thin.
I have unraveled.

Sleep
arrives too late
to save me from myself
or from you.

The Poem She Would Like to Have Read at Forty

Her friend Vicki issued a writing challenge:
"Respond to this prompt –
She could not decide whether to use her poems for good or for evil."

Could she answer the challenge with the
Great American Divorce poem—
the one that reminds you to follow your heart
as you make the tough decisions,
and confirms it is not only possible
but also permissible
to walk away from a marriage
after five or seventeen or thirty years of trying to make it work?

She paused at Frost's diverging roads
            and considered her poetic options.

The evil road presented itself.
She could simply rant about his self-loathing and anger.
She could tell about his letting the car insurance lapse
without informing her,
or how every time he lost his keys (or his wallet, or his job)
someone else was to blame.
She could recite the litany of dark moods,
destructive behaviors,
and desperate apologies
(delivered, it's true, with flowers, trout amandine, and
chardonnay),
or narrate her attempts to make him take responsibility
as she waited
while he left his glass one-third full of orange juice
on the dresser
where it sat for days

weeks
the liquid becoming increasingly rancid,
filling the room with sour acidity.
She could reveal the time he
accidentally
left the car running all night in the closed garage
forcing carbon monoxide fumes
into the children's lungs and rooms
so that in the morning they both awoke
groggy, listless,
complaining of headaches
and nausea
and how she, incredulous, took them to the emergency room
for blood draws and oxygen.

Then she decided to write for good,
for her friends living through the pain of indecision
and the grief of loss that lingers
when dreams dissolve into nightmares,
or nothingness.
It would do them good, she thought,
to know that quicksand will not swallow them whole
nor will the mountain peak elude them forever.
She would write the poem she would like to have read
when at forty
she screamed one long keening syllable
that rose from her bowels and belly and throat
emerging high and loud and clear
"NOooooooooo!"

The Great American Divorce poem
could free her friends from guilt and remorse,
blame and sorrow,
free them from inside the opaque bubble.
And free him, too, perhaps.

Yes, she would use her poem for good,
reminding herself and others
to breathe
as waterfalls cascade down steep granite faces
into canyons alive with flame maple and trail orchids.
Breathe
as the snow melts in the yellow wood.

Breathe.

The Dark Side of Missing

Each year
        leaves fall
        light fades
and winter swallows you into its belly
beyond reach.

Oh, how I miss you—
miss us—
in these tall grey hours

of depressed silence.

You disappear
into the black recesses of O'Keeffe's New York street

leaving me alone
with her iron street lamp,
its faint pulse
  the only evidence that
   we
exist.

Night Visitors

The yellow moon appeared last night.
Peering through the bedroom window,
he woke me
as I tried to reclaim my disturbed rest.

Insistent,
he sat on the edge of my bed
then spread across my feet and legs.
His jaundiced eye perceived the vacant space
        beside me—
  the untouched pillow
  and smooth sheets.
His lips curved into a sly smile
before he slid past the door.

No sooner had he slipped away,
then a tiny red velvet spider appeared
on the nightstand
very near to my ear.
In a silky voice
she whispered a poisonous tale
spinning a web with filaments of
loneliness and fear.

As she repelled on her thread
I lay still in the dark
my head filled with phantoms
until sleep won
and Yeats arrived
a marble triton, wise with years
and a rose in his heart.

We sailed away on a sad sea
to a distant shore
where you greeted us

and took my hand.

Contemplation

A breeze stirs the warm evening.

The tattered beach towel
clings to the curtain rod
where Ruthie had tied it
days ago
when she moved in.

From her bed across the room,
she ponders the faded pattern.
Sun-bleached tropical fish
swim through curved
columns of seaweed
on this thin, dulled remnant of her childhood.

Tired of unpacking old boxes
of older belongings
again
Ruthie dozes.

A sudden midnight storm
bursts through the bedroom window.
The towel snaps Ruthie awake.

One corner still tethered to the bare rod,
the rest floating and flapping in the wind,
the threadbare towel becomes
an intoxicated woman
her arm draped luxuriously
around a slender man's neck,
her head and body swaying unevenly

as he leads her
into the shadows.

Ruthie had never seen
or been
such a woman,
but she knew her now,
hanging
                in the window.

My Las Vegas

That night, after tucking you into bed, I rendezvoused with Dwight, Jean Paul, and all their friends at The Mirage where I was dubbed "Vanessa" for the evening; later we found ourselves on Fremont Street, dazzled by the arcing light show and the fantastic parade of tourists, gamblers, and newlyweds. We played the nickel slots and lost. Finally, we ended up on a round hotel bed, staring up at the mirrored ceiling, and laughing about my phoning to tell you I would be spending the night with two queens. I drove your car home to Henderson,
    instead.

Following an evening visit with you last fall, I returned to my conference hotel and wanted to cry. Instead, I walked to Caesar's, and wandered into a cheap Italian restaurant whose waiter apologetically brought me an advertisement for a strip club (blank on the back) and a Keno crayon—all he could find in response to my request for something to write with while waiting for my ravioli and Shiraz. When the piano man played a Nora Jones tune, her lyrics rolled themselves toward me like glass beads: "don't know why I didn't come...." But I had come, to see you, and now I was failing to hide my pain from the attentive, handsome Arab waiter whose dark eyes spoke sympathy
    and more.

I hate Las Vegas, this toxic wasteland of blinking dinging slot machines, cigarette smoke, all-you-can eat buffets, and implausibilities like penguins swimming outside the desert Flamingo. But here I am, waiting impatiently in the afternoon shimmer and glitz for a ride from your friends Abe and Bea instead of taking a taxi. Only in Vegas can you stand at the curb under a palm tree next to the Eiffel Tower. A woman at the nearby bus stop tells me I'll get snatched up soon if my ride doesn't hurry up.

"You're a beautiful woman," she says. I want to tell her I look like you, but she wouldn't
  understand.

Do you remember our family vacation to Vegas when I was a little girl? We stayed at the Golden Key Motel. You and dad got all dressed up and went out on the town to relive your glamorous honeymoon, leaving me with Laura and Jeff, the three of us alone in the room watching the Smothers Brothers' Comedy Hour. I played on the bed with a golden-haired blue-eyed doll I named Angel, a gift from you to keep me quiet
  and happy.

I'm rarely happy in Vegas now, in this Vegas of hospice nurses and a hostile stepfather and too much time to think at the Southwest Airlines departure gates where I sit now, so tired and hurting from catching you this morning as you fell backwards out of your walker, still gripping the refrigerator door handle, trying to steady yourself while the door pulled open and I raced across the tile floor to catch you before you, in slow motion, yielded completely to gravity. My back spasms in pain and frustration, while my heart knows only that my mother, my steady guide, will never again stand up for herself, recover her balance, or glitter gracefully in
  my Las Vegas.

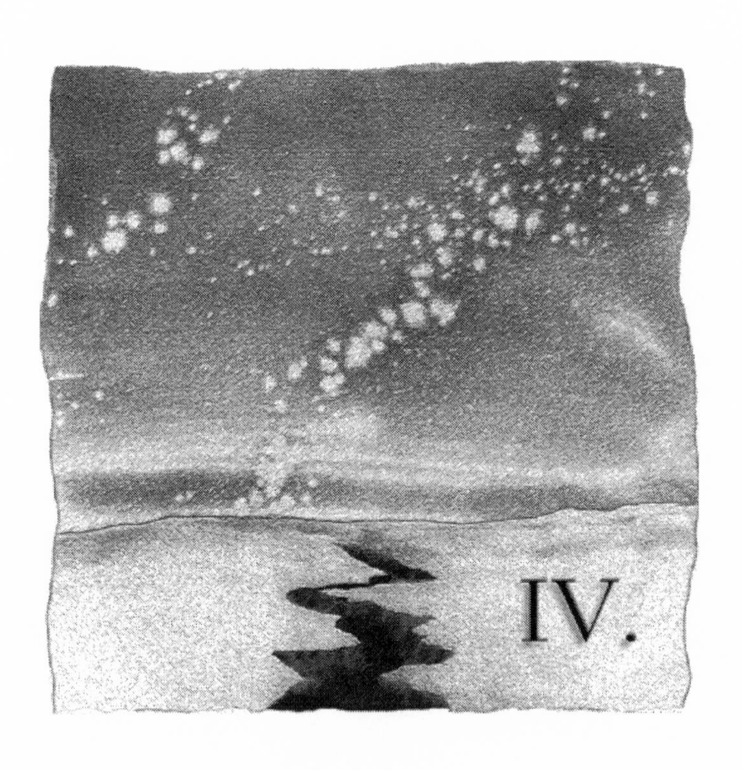
IV.

You don't have to understand what is happening. But remember this day. You will recognize it later. You are part of it now.

- Leslie Silko

BUT NOT TODAY

Peace Talks

For the woman interviewed on NPR
after the fourth suicide bomb attack.

Every other day we go to the market,
    every other day we go out in public.
We take the bus and go to the shops.
But not today,
    for some reason, not today.
Today we should have gone
    my baby and I
    we should have gone.
But we didn't,
    we stayed home.
My baby and I, we stayed home.

And if we had gone
    to the shops today—

Oh my God! If we had gone today....
For some reason we did not go.
For some reason my baby and I stayed home.
My God—
    what is happening here?

The Last Days

These are the last days
of summer
when children sit on fences
and smoke menthol cigarettes stolen
　　　　from their mother's purses
when a graying veteran rides circles through the
　　　　neighborhood
balancing his pet parrot on the handlebars
and when lovers hold hands
　　　　on front porches
　　　　or back steps
lingering in the dying
　　　　pink glow of sunset
　　　　watching for the first stars
all
knowing it could well be
their last night together
　　　　or alone.

After dark
televisions glow blue
in neighborhood living rooms.

A woman stops ironing shirts
and stands attentively
as the dead soldiers' photographs appear
　　　　eleven
　　　　tonight
each with a name, age, rank
　　　　and home town—
some, with an incongruous smile.

Coming Across

I do not understand you americans
why you say things you do not mean
I read about you before I came
the book said
        When an american says
                come on over sometime
        he doesn't mean it
I came over anyway
I crossed an ocean to get here
and now I've crossed the street
will you let me in? I do not understand why
but I will continue to ask
        How are you?
        and not wait for an answer
        like you do
if it makes you feel better
I'll even keep talking
so you can try to imitate my accent
which you seem to find so amusing
but what I really want
is to learn from you
not just take classes in your university
to get inside your red, white, and blue
I want you to listen
and to learn from me
not just my recipes from home
or my native costume
but my culture, my politics, my religion....
and my loves, my family, my self.

Can you even find my country on a map?

Letters to Prison

When you're seventeen
  you don't know any better,
so when you read a personal ad
  in the *Daily Nexus*
—Pen Pal Wanted—
you write a letter
even though the name
has a long number after it
and the P.O. Box address
in Lompoc, California
follows the words
"Minimum Security."

You're excited when the first letter arrives
  from B53728
but you know
from the code stamped in black ink
inside the envelope
you're not the first one to read its contents.

In colored pencil
he's drawn you a picture of a teddy bear
with a heart on its chest inscribed
    "Please Bear With Me"
and because you're seventeen
you think it's cute and sad.

He tells you how much he misses
his family in Iowa,
his old blue Camaro convertible,
and his buddies, outside,
Signed,
    Your Friend.

You write back
    in your best handwriting
    adding a few little flourishes—
            a smiley face here,
            a star, there.

You tell him all about school
    your courses, your roommate,
    the dorm, the dining hall.
You never hint at family matters
            like divorce, mental illness, alcoholism—
trying to stay upbeat
for his sake.

After a few months
of weekly correspondence
he asks you to send a Christmas package. You agree.
He sends you the mailing instructions,
an authorization form, and a list of allowable items:
            beef jerky
            slim-jim sausages
            smoked cheese
            Hershey's chocolate bars (no nuts)

After final exams,
    you hitch a ride home with friends,
    and stay at your mom's.
Once home, you buy all the food
    and put it carefully in a box.
But you get lazy or busy and forget to mail it
until the last day of the year.

Back at school,
    a letter is waiting.
January 10.

B53278 is upset.
You can tell by his handwriting,
small, tight script in dark, smeared pencil.

He says that because of you,
he got nothing for Christmas.
If you'd bothered to read the instructions,
you'd have known he's allowed only one package per month.
Yours was supposed to arrive in December.
It didn't.
The prison refused delivery
of his sister's January care package because
your box got there the day before.
And you're supposed to be a college student. Can't you read?

His anger frightens you,
and for the first time you wonder why he's in prison,
and when he'll get out.

You cry.
You write a short apology,
thinking he probably never wants
to hear from you again...
praying he never writes you another letter.

But spring arrives
along with hope, forgiveness, and a letter from B53278.

You turn eighteen and write to him about your party.
You offer to send him an Easter box,
but he says
never mind.

Then months of silence.

A thick envelope appears.
You recognize the handwriting,
and the number,
but the San Quentin address is new.

He did a stupid thing – he confesses.
Got into it with a guard.
They transferred him to
Maximum Security,
starting with a couple of months
in Solitary
He wants out of his hell-hole
And he thinks he knows how.

You don't want to know.
Not today.
Not ever.

Dilemma

A child of evening news body counts,
I had hoped my own children
might never, in their youth,
see the U.S. at war.
But over a decade ago,
at age 5, my daughter tied yellow ribbons to the schoolyard fence
and learned to spell Iraq.

Now, at 18, she calls from college—
"I'm writing this paper and I'm stuck.
Can you help me?"
We talk about Hamlet's
moral dilemma in Act III, scene iii:
murder for revenge?

The next day,
our President moves
Us closer to war,

and Erin emails a draft of her paper, saying:
I'm having trouble with the resolution.

So am I.

How Was Your Weekend?

For Cynthia, after her phone call

How was your weekend?
I asked.
My grandpa almost froze to death
last Saturday night, after the snow,
she said.

Auntie came over and woke me up.
Said she'd seen him outside, stumbling,
when she drove back from bingo.
Shit, I said.

I always watch him,
but sometimes I'm gone
          at school or somewhere
and I can't watch him.

Couldn't find him, either.
Walked back up the road
and stopped at Rooster's house.
The lights were on.
Rooster and Albert came out
into the dark
with flashlights.

I finally found him in a bush
asleep, cold
drunk off his ass.
He drinks when he gets his checks.
He'll drink for a week if no one stops him.

Rooster and Albert called ALC.*
Got an ambulance.
Grandpa was still passed out
when they took him.
I was cold and tired.
I just wanted to sleep.
Shit, she said.

**Acoma-Laguna-Cañoncito Hospital*

Loraine Gold Mine No. 2 Shaft

Republic of South Africa, 1980

My new pen friend, *he wrote,*
I was very glad to receive your letter
from California. You are the only
college student I know.

What is it like, Santa Barbara?

I am a real Mosotho (Black man)
          born in Lesotho.

Now I am
an immigrant laborer.
I have not yet marry
          (I am 28)
but it is my intention to marry
whenever I have enough money.

I am left with my mother (a widow)
          and two brothers and one sister.
I like music—pop, very much.
I like to read books
and watch tennis and football.

I work in a mine.
I am an underground worker most of the time.
Sometimes   we come out.
Underground is a very dangerous place.
One or two people die per day.
But when I work
          I forget everything.

We work with whites
in a very hot place and too much dark.
Sometimes   you can be lost for two or three weeks.
We go down
in a cage
and out also
by it.
The cage is a risk
            because it can become broken.
            Most people in it would die.

I am not happy in this place
but because I am moneyless,
I have to stay.
Every two or three months
I visit home.

I cannot say too much
about whites in our area—
just a few facts.

First, at the end of month,
we blacks get fifty dollars
while whites get one to two thousand per month
as a salary
            but our work is same.

We (blacks) are always called dogs
and other bad names
by whites.
We cannot eat or stay with them.

But I will say more when you answer me.

Now what I want to know is

are you she or he?
I am also sure that I will get your picture,
then I gonna be glad and happy.

I wish you nice Christmas and good New Year.

I am not going to give you my full name.
I have written some facts
which can lead me to jail
as you know South Africa.

Still, I think you remember me.

Your Mosotho pen pal.

The Franchise

Before I make the long drive home in early autumn darkness,
My daughter and I meet between her classes for afternoon coffee.

While she digs for dollar bills and comes up empty,
I watch the cash register item-display
...Tall Latte $2.95
Pumpkin Bread $1.85...
WAIT, I protest to the cashier.
That should be one-SEVENTY-five.
No, she says. The computer rang it up for one-EIGHTY-five.
I see that, but the bakery case sign clearly reads
Seasonally Delicious Pumpkin Bread $1.75

There's nothing I can do, she says. We had a price increase,
but we haven't received new signs from Corporate.
(Toothy, vacuous smile followed by hair toss.)

Appealing to her moral center, I suggest
You can make a new sign yourself to avoid future
false advertising.

We're not allowed to alter their signs,
So there's really nothing I can do.

While my brain tries to calculate the Corporate profit
earned when every customer
who celebrates the delicious pumpkin season
is overcharged ten cents,
Erin glides away from me,
toward the Pick-Up Order Here counter,
distancing herself again from my principal-of-the-thing outrage.

I can't resist one last attempt as I hand over my cash.
You CAN do something, I assert.
You can give me an extra dime.

The register drawer pops open –
She counts back the change for my ten dollar bill
exactly as the computer tells her to
Plus ten cents more.

I smile, tossing the dime into the tip jar.
There is something
I can do.

War Zone Moon

A translucent body bathed
and dressed in sheer blue morning light,
she floats
above our stifling afternoon
opposite her daytime lover
on his glowing throne.

Her elegant curved hips
and porcelain lips
mock our plodding
steps
and
heavy, draped bellies.

We crave her celestial serenity
as we trudge home
burdened by
our husbands' untimely absence.

While we await
their safe return
she sails placidly through blue haze
like a goddess
toward her purple bed
and ancient starry conquests
so far from this tortured earth.

V.

FORBIDDEN FRUITS
MAKE MANY JAMS

~ Church marquee, Farmington, New Mexico

Forbidden Fruit Jam

If

Sometimes
I
slow
right
down
and
stop

to
rub a branch of rosemary,
snap a sprig of sage,
pick up a penny,
or
glance
at a man
in a parking lot.

Might miss him
if
I
walk
too
fast.

Reflection

Absently caressing the pine countertop.
I stare past your kitchen window
into the garden of blossoming blue rosemary
          and life-sized stone sculptures—
          naked, faceless forms.

My fingers trace a whorled knot of lust and self-doubt.

One foot poised on the barstool,
I shift my weight
and my gaze
only to discover your reflection in the pane—
          arms crossed, waiting.

I close my hands around your warm orange coffee mug,
Acutely aware
as you assess my hips, my back, my hair.

I freeze with dread
          when I hear my name.

Near the Library

Our paths crossed at a distance yesterday.
Carefully avoiding puddles, you didn't
catch my eye across the campus lawn.
I almost called out,
to let you know how close I really was,
but swallowed the impulse.
Instead, I followed your corduroy stride
and enjoyed your crooked smile,
unobserved.

You picked up a floating yellow leaf,
ran your fingers along its contoured edges,
and placed it gently into a book.

Think of me, when you find it again—
            tucked away, waiting.

Rafaello

Do you still keep me upstairs
on that shelf—
    above the faded loveseat
    next to the small birch bookcase
there with your spare glasses,
old calendars, paper clips,
and notepads made from the drafts of unfinished stories?

Returning a borrowed novel
I had felt naked when I saw my letter —
folded pages
separated slightly   exposed.

I wanted to snatch the white sheets,
    but your sudden footsteps startled me.

I continued editing your manuscript
while sipping cappuccino
sighing often
    while you made love to me
        in your dreams.

Today, I awaken to my own dream.

The iron stove warms the studio.
    Kneeling in front of the open glow,
    I break branches between my
    fingers and feed them to the flames.
        From behind, you select more slender boughs
    for me to snap,
        one after another,
        into the red, enveloping heat.

Then you hand me the letter.

We watch it disintegrate to ash
before we shut the door.

JEANS

I wish things were different between us.
Between us—
nothing yet everything in the way
of our satisfying, painful loving.

What's that old song—
"If loving you is wrong, I don't want to be right"? Yep.

Oh well.
Someday I'll have it all
and this will seem like a favorite old pair of faded jeans
that just doesn't fit anymore.

Damn, you look good in jeans.

Things that Melt

Ice
Butter
Wax
Snow

Years
Glaciers
Distances
Me,
  in your arms.

School's Out

We walked from her house
taking turns with the aluminum bucket, giggling and
shivering as cold water sloshed onto our sandaled white feet.

Yesterday had been spring and eighth grade,
but today we dared the sun to burn our sleeveless forearms
and bare legs
on our first day of freedom.

We went the "back way"— through the orange grove
where the boys had pelted us with sticky rotten Valencias,
over the wire fence, carefully
          first me, then the bucket, then her

past the driveway leading to the old ladies' two-story
white Victorian,
(fearing the spinster sisters who spied on us through lace
curtains
          that time we stole their pomegranates and ran)

now into the alley whose cinderblock wall hid us
from the pickers' view
and finally, slowly, crouching
across a small muddy ditch into the adjacent field,
a shimmering sea of green
          dotted with straw hats.

She set down the bucket and began to search the plants,
her fingers deftly separating the leaves to reveal the prize:
          red, ripe, juicy strawberries
          huge cultivated fruit—our wild suburban treasure.

Cars whisked past. A few slowed up the distant dirt driveway
then stopped at the whitewashed shack advertising
S T R A W B E R R I E S in dripping red

but she ignored them, picking fruit quickly
placing each berry gently into the cool water
while I searched for the ripest sweetest reddest ones.

"Look up," she said suddenly.
My face followed my eyes to meet hers hazel, sparkling.
Between her thumb and juice-stained fingers she held
a scarlet jewel
by its stem poised waiting for me
to open my mouth
to take my first taste
of summer.

The Glass-Bowl Offering

Expectant Sarah sits on pillows
surrounded by a large circle of women
who have come to celebrate
her fertile essence.

The host begins: Into this water, I have placed
a crystal for clarity, saffron for strength
and lavender for love.

Let us embrace Sarah by offering to remove her fears,
to bear their weight,
so she may bear her child in complete peace and power.
Sarah, I take your fear of the unknown.

The woman to her left accepts the bowl, and speaks,
Sarah, I take your fear of not making it to the hospital in time.
The next, a young mother, asserts,
I take your fear of making mistakes.

Saffron swirls in warm stirred spirals
each woman voices ancient and modern anxieties
before passing the glass bowl.

I take your fear of illness, disease, deformity, and death.
I take your fear of not knowing what to do when your baby cries.

Sarah listens to each woman
speak unnamed worries
and name unspoken fears.

I take your fear of a labor too long, or too short.
I take your fear of how your body will look
after the baby is born.

Clockwise around the room the bowl moves, passed
    among women of all ages, shapes, and hair colors,
    each one exposing and expelling fear.

Sarah sighs and adjusts herself on the cushion.

I take your fear of not having the support you need
    when you move away this summer.
I take your fear of how others will judge you as a mother.

Sarah frowns, not one to invite confrontation.

I'll take any fear you want to name, says the brave
    mother of three.

    Sarah says: Okay, then I'm afraid my boobs will leak!
    The fear dissolves into laughter.

I take your fear of spiders and insects,
and all creatures that crawl and hop and fly. They can't harm
    you, or the baby,
says the biologist who believes in leprechauns.

Sarah's mother proclaims:
I take your fear that your mother will come live with you!

Sarah smiles.

I take your fear of being a bad mother.
I take your fear of never reading a book, seeing a movie,
or having an adult conversation again.

When all the women have spoken Sarah's fears
she receives the bowl and stirs the water
fearless
anticipating her newborn with clarity, strength, and love.

A Fantasy in Six Parts

I. Wanting to
come
home
because you're there

II. Slipping
into a sleeping bag
under the stars
sliding, colliding
into you

III. Mountain meadow
wildflowers
warm sun
cool breeze
no bugs
biting
you, me

IV. Library
Sssshhhh
stealing kisses
in the stacks
tasting you
in the
PRs
PNs
PSs

V. Strip
of beach
waves
warm, salty, wet
crashing
repeatedly

VI. Crackling fire
port
books
chenille throws
lingering
'til dawn
fingering
you

Katherine, Northern Territory

Dizzy with cabernet
at the Barra Café
waiting for fish and chips
between adventures
I scribble a few postcards.

Monday found us far from Darwin,
alone and naked on Cassaurina Beach
at sunset's low tide
a quarter-mile from the shore
looking west toward Madagascar—
if only we could see across six thousand miles
of ocean and sky.

Yesterday we counted cockatoos and crocodiles
on the misnamed East Alligator River
while our Guluyambi guides
shared survival stories.

Last night in our bush bungalow
we listened to a bat song serenade
before succumbing to dreams of long jaws and swishing tails.

Today we breathed the smoke of bush fires
surrounding aboriginal settlements.
40,000 years of survival hung in hot, humid silence.
Remote rock overhangs and human caretakers
protect ancient depictions of Lightning Man and Rainbow Snake
Kangaroos and Barramundi.

Tonight—
love on a soft bed

in Katherine, officially a Tidy Town,
the ceiling fan hum harmonizes
with Victoria Highway's rumbling road trains.
Extra pillows
a luxury.

Confluence

We once flowed
in different directions
through years and layers
sands and sediment

each one carrying
alluvial debris, uprooted trees,
smooth boulders, dead leaves.

Now our waters meet in foam,
tumbling into one another—
cool, quick green
colliding with warm, slow brown.

We mix uneasily at first,
roiling hungrily
drawn together, rushing downstream
as we are pulled forward by forces
primordial and eternal
in a timeless wild dance
at the confluence.

Knowing You

I have seen the green river in your eyes
And heard the weariness of travel in your strained voice.

I have tasted the salt on your shoulders
And smelled the bay laurel on your fingertips.

I have watched you suck a blood orange in a California grove
And listened to you breathe in the New Mexico dawn.

I have witnessed your devotion to doing good and doing it well
And touched your eyelids as you dreamed constellations and comets.

I have seen you delight in scampering quail and resting deer
And heard the wine cork pop after your steady pull.

I have admired your strong legs, fresh from a morning run
And felt your long arms enfold me with quiet strength.

I have perceived your pleasure and your pain
And know that I have been both.

Dance Envy in Austin

At Antone's
musicians gather on the stage
testing their sound
asking the faceless booth, "Where's Joe?"
ignoring the audience.

I watch a woman seated nearby.

Even with averted gaze
through smoky haze
I can tell
she's a dancer.

Legs outstretched on a chair in front of her,
a loose skirt flows off her calves
over flat, strappy leather sandals.

Bare arms fold gracefully across her belly.

Her brown wavy hair cascades down her back.
She's unadorned—no makeup, no jewelry—
luminous in blue energy.

I'm drawn to her
as to a distant relative whose sepia mirror image
I discover in an old family photo album.

Joe arrives
large and loud
in bright yellow tennis shoes and long dreads.

As he grabs the microphone and belts out the blues

the dancer's foot gently moves
in slow time with her nodding head.

You keep telling me to go, mama,
But there's a man down there
He might be yo' man
I don't know.

I close my eyes
imagining the scene a few weeks ago
when Antone died
and mourners and musicians arrived
with candles, flowers, and photographs
all still on display
separated from the stage by a black velvet curtain.

She's disappeared, my dancer—
her sandals on the floor
dropped casually—

Then I spot her swaying near the black curtain
apart from the crowd of sweaty couples
hips circling loosely above bare feet
eyes focused on a distant memory
lips parted in a sultry smile.

She moves
like I want to,
dances
like I know I could.

Forbidden Fruit Jam

Sunday's sermon title
on the Baptist Church sign
sternly warns:

FORBIDDEN FRUITS
MAKE MANY JAMS.

As I drive past,
my thoughts ripen
toward luscious, lickable loganberry lips,
and sweet, dark cherry syrup
finger-spread across your
  tongue.

Our table is laden with fresh figs and dates,
 lychee and kumquat.
Golden grape clusters spill over platters
 of persimmon, quince, orange, and lime.

In the steamy kitchen
you peel soft skin
from round ripe peaches
while I pare the zest of citrus rinds
until our hands
preserve the scent of pleasure.

Exotic fruit flesh bubbles
 into thick aromas.
You kiss the marmalade sweat
 from my neck and brow—

Oh, don't stop now—

Keep stirring our wild raspberry-rhubarb passion
until the perfect full rolling boil
draws me in sticky sheets
and we can keep
the lid
on this jar
no longer.

Unintentionally evoking
the tangy spice
of our illicit mango love,
that preacher will never know
the delicious truth
of his marquee's message.

About the Author

Andrea (Andi) Millenson Penner sees the world through the places where she has lived – from Connecticut to Southern California, and Northern Arizona to Central and Northwest New Mexico. She knows those places through the people she has met and the relationships she has formed, and left behind. Andi's educational journey led her to many of the locations featured in her poetry. After high school, Andi left her childhood home in Orange County to pursue her B. A. in Developmental Psychology at the University of California Santa Barbara.

Following a domestic era, she continued with graduate school, earning an M.A. in English at Northern Arizona University in Flagstaff. Relocating to Albuquerque, she engaged in a multi-year juggling act while completing doctoral study in Native American Literature and earning the PhD in English at the University of New Mexico. She has taught composition, literature, and technical writing at her graduate alma maters and at San Juan College. She has also worked in private industry and traveled abroad. She writes and lives in Albuquerque, New Mexico, a favorite place.

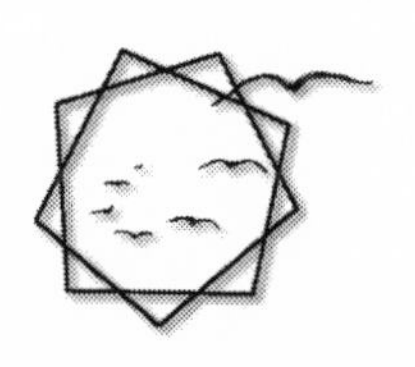

Made in the USA
Charleston, SC
09 October 2013